The Bourne Society

THEN AND NOW
The Changing Scene
of
Surrey Life
in
Coulsdon & Purley

The cover photograph c.1904
shows Brighton Road, Purley,
at the junction with Purley Road.

First Published 1989
© The Bourne Society 1989
All Rights Reserved. No Reproduction
Permitted Without The Prior Permission
Of the Publishers:
The Bourne Society
17 Manor Avenue,
Caterham, Surrey
CR3 6AP

ISBN 0-900992-30-1

Typeset and Printed by Lyndhurst Printing Company Limited
Hardley Industrial Estate, Hythe, Southampton SO4 6ZX

Printed in England

FOREWORD

Councillor Stanley E. Littlechild

I am sure that everyone who reads this publication will appreciate the time and thought that The Bourne Society has given to this study.

My wife and I moved to Old Coulsdon in 1933. Since 1939 I have been an elected local government member for the district. During this time I have witnessed the transformation from a mainly rural area to a developed urban district that is now part of The London Borough of Croydon.

I can recall much of the opposition to the growth and development of the area. I am also vividly aware of the human pleasure that the development has given to the families who are now living in the district.

Planning officers are aware that their decisions are usually welcomed by some, though often vigorously opposed by others. The growth of a district calls for careful preservation of the past while satisfying the needs of the day, therefore a balance has to be sought. Perhaps the important consideration should be to conserve the natural aspect, particularly trees and the habitat, thus creating a pleasant balance between nature and human habitation.

S E Littlechild

S.E. LITTLECHILD

1989

PREFACE

The success of our original 'Then and Now' book, which covered the whole of The Bourne Society area, prompted us to embark on a more extensive coverage of Coulsdon and Purley.

None of our efforts would have been worthwhile without the skill and dedication of those early photographers, who at the beginning of this century, spent so much time recording the area in great detail.

Their equipment was heavy and bulky, but despite these disadvantages they produced photographs of both technical and pictorial quality, that even today with modern light-weight and automatic cameras are difficult to surpass. As this year is the 150th anniversary of photography, it is appropriate to dedicate our book to those early pioneers.

Grahame W. Brooks

SOURCES

The information in this publication has been obtained from many sources. Anyone wishing to study in more depth should find the following publications of interest;
Local History Records - The Bourne Society.
Coulsdon in Old Picture Postcards - Roger Packham - European Library.
The Caterham Railway - Jeoffry Spence - The Oakwood Press.
Coulsdon Downland Village - The Bourne Society.
The Royal Russell School - A History - S. Hopewell.

It is inevitable in producing a publication of this kind that errors and omissions will occur. We apologise for any that may be found and would welcome comments from readers.

ACKNOWLEDGEMENTS

The task of producing this book was undertaken by the following members of the Photographic Group;

Grahame Brooks, Ronald Dabbs, Roger Hammond, Roger Packham, Paul Sandford, Ivon Teear and Dorothy Tutt.

Acknowledgement is also due to many members and friends of the Society who gave help and advice;

Mr. Roger Packham for lending the postcards from his collection.
Mr. Len Muggeridge for drawing the maps of Coulsdon and Purley.
Miss M. Conlan and the pupils of Thomas More School
Mr. Maurice Cooke
Mrs. Mary Saaler
Mr. John Gent
Mr. Jeoffry Spence
The staff of Purley Reference Library

INTRODUCTION

The first of our 'Then and Now' publications was planned deliberately to present in a few pages what could be called a 'taster' for each of the principal places within the area covered by the Bourne Society. In this way we created a book which has proved to be of interest to residents throughout the district. This, our second volume, covers only what in 1989 is known as Purley and Coulsdon. Modern Kenley was, of course, within the ancient boundary of Coulsdon, but space does not permit its inclusion in this volume.

The Urban District of Coulsdon and Purley came into being in 1915, being previously part of Croydon Rural District. Boundary changes in 1929, and again in 1933, greatly increased the area administered by the Coulsdon & Purley Urban District Council. With the implementation of the more recent changes in 1965, the eighteen square miles covering Coulsdon, Purley, Hooley, Kenley, Sanderstead, Selsdon and Farleigh, became overnight the southern part of the new London Borough of Croydon. Farleigh protested, putting forward a strong legal case, and in 1968 won its freedom, returning to Godstone Rural District, now incorporated into Tandridge District. Hooley also managed to escape from the newly formed London Borough.

Coulsdon is the only ancient village settlement still existing in the area. John Rocque's map, of late 18th century date, shows a considerable network of what would have been rough roads and trackways. Some are now principal routes, while others have altered or disappeared. The farms were well scattered, being situated, with the exception of Purley Farm and Stoats Nest, on the higher ground well out of the valley. The Red Lion Inn stands at an important junction called Leaden Cross, later Lion Green. The Church in the old village of Coulsdon had a large parish but a small population. In 1801 there were 420 people in 4314 acres.

In the 19th century the peace of the valley was first disturbed by the construction of a horse drawn tramway, extending the Surrey Iron Railway as far as Merstham Quarries. This was in use from 1805, but a much greater disturbance was soon to follow with the construction of the London & Brighton Railway Company's line which opened as far as Haywards Heath in 1841. A station was opened, named Godstone Road, and another further south at Stoats Nest. However, little or no house building resulted, and the Godstone Road Station closed in 1847 due to lack of custom. Renamed Caterham Junction, it reopened in 1856 when the branch line along the valley in the direction of Godstone was constructed. Thereafter some new building did start, though very slowly at first. Stoats Nest station was closed to passengers in 1856.

On a nearby hill Reedham Orphanage, later School, was built. It had been founded in 1844, and the building, opened in 1858, was demolished in 1980. Across the valley, on another hill, 1866 brought the opening of the new buildings of the Warehousemen, Clerks and Drapers' School, which had been founded by Lord John Russell in 1863. The tollgate on the road at Foxley Hatch was abolished in 1865, and by 1877 there were enough people living in this now expanding area by the railway to need a local church. Completed in 1878 it was initially a chapel of ease to St. John's, Coulsdon, but in 1884 the separate parish of Christ Church, Purley was formed. In 1988 the station was officially renamed Purley, and a plaque commemorating this event has been placed on the station façade by the Bourne Society.

Further south, in 1883 the London County Council purchased the Portnalls Estate. Cane Hill Asylum was built, and soon houses and shops began to spread along the road around the Red Lion. Sadly, the open space called Lion Green was lost forever. A second branch railway line from Purley opened to Kingswood in 1897. Stations added later were Smitham (1904) and Reedham (1911). On the main line a new station, now called Coulsdon South, opened in 1889. Electric trams came to Purley in 1901, and the first motor bus (London General Omnibus Co.) came through to the Red Lion in 1913.

Meanwhile, although building had been spreading for some years along Smitham Bottom, (the old name for the valley from southern Croydon to Lion Green), up on the hill Coulsdon Village saw little change. Edmund Byron still controlled his quite extensive estate, and did not die until 1921. Thereafter the land was sold, much of it for building. So, in what is known as Old Coulsdon to distinguish it from the modern development in the valley, there are some fine old buildings and a few built by the Byrons in the 19th century, but the greater part date from around 1930 onwards.

Mention must be made of the Coulsdon Bourne, a natural flow of water now contained below ground but which used to cause much flooding, especially just south of the Red Lion. At Purley this movement of water combines with a similar flow from the Caterham Valley. Until the late 1930s this stream could be seen in an open ditch between Purley High Street and the Brighton Road as it made its way to help form the Wandle, and so to the Thames.

These few parargraphs have endeavoured to set the scene for you, and whether resident or a visitor to Coulsdon and Purley we are sure you will find much of interest in this book.

Dorothy Tutt

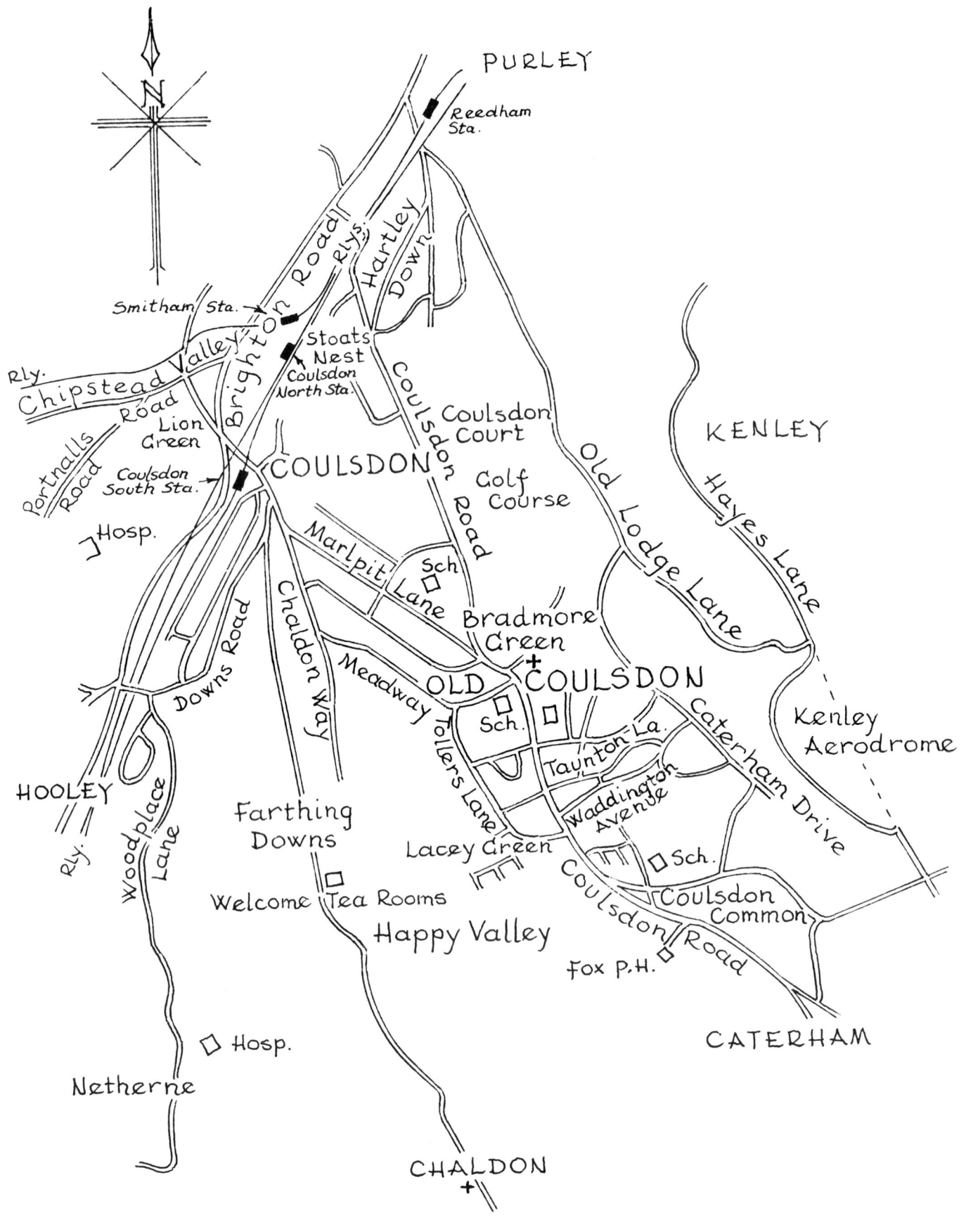

Coulsdon

With Every Good Wish From COULSDON

Best of Luck, Best of Health, Happiness and enough of wealth Prosperous times, Pleasant days With fortune as your Friend always.

The parish of Coulsdon has changed dramatically during the present century. From the isolated buildings around St John's Church and some recently developed housing on the Brighton Road at Smitham, the transformation occurred largely between the wars following the death of Edmund Byron, (last Lord of the Manor of Coulsdon), in 1921 and the sale of his estate. The Tudor style housing on the hill has matured into the present-day village of Old Coulsdon and building in the Smitham valley has also increased. At the time of writing there is considerable pressure to build a large housing estate in the grounds of Cane Hill.

It is hoped that this series of 'Then and Now' photographs will convey something of the great changes that have occurred during the century and give the reader some idea of how the parish appeared before the large-scale alterations took place.

Old Post Office, Bradmore Green, Coulsdon.

These two Edwardian views show the Coulsdon Post Office when it was situated at Cherry Tree Cottage, now a private residence close to Stanley Close on the Coulsdon Road. It was also the village stores and had been an ale house and the headquarters of the Coulsdon Cricket Club who played their matches on the ground at the back. The old lady is standing in front of an old advertisement for R. White's Lemonade and Ginger Beer.

Cherry Tree Cottage is again featured in these two views as it appeared in the early 1930s and at the present day. In the earlier view it is still serving as the Post Office and Village Stores before the building of the parade of shops next to the Tudor Rose.

The other house shown is Pound Cottage, for many years the home of Mr F.H.B. Ellis, a Coulsdon councillor and former Chairman of Coulsdon & Purley Council, who was aware of the changing nature of the locality and set about to record it for posterity with a series of evocative photographs.

9

The Pond, Bradmore Green, Coulsdon, Surrey.

Some thirsty cattle are pleased to drink from Bradmore Pond in about 1905.

In recent years much effort has been made towards restoration of the pond which is a valuable feature of the Conservation Area. The buildings of Bradmore Farm appear to be in a much better state of maintenance in the modern photograph.

A 1920s motor car passes Grange Park, Old Coulsdon in the years preceding the construction of The Tudor Parade.

In the top photograph St. John's Church and lych-gate and Church Path Cottages may just be seen on the left-hand side. Note the matching of the gables in the newly built Dormer Lodge on the right of the modern photograph.

St. John's Church, Old Coulsdon is featured here as it appeared in 1912 and 1989.

The two mature trees and iron fences have disappeared and the more recent photograph shows the modern extension on the south side of the Church which was built in 1957-1959.

The 1930s view shows the recent development of the Tudor Estate and is looking towards Court Avenue from Placehouse Lane, with Coulsdon Road running left to right of the picture. The Tudor Rose public house is out of sight on the far right.

The estate agent's house has been re-built and it is doubtful whether the prices shown in the earlier photograph (£595 or £750 for freehold properties) would be believed by the present employees.

The Village Smithy - Coulsdon

These photographs show the Coulsdon Road at Lacey Green looking towards Coulsdon Common with the earlier one dating from about 1908.

The old smithy has given way to the City Petrol Station and shops but it is reassuring that one of the chestnut trees remains on the corner of Waddington Avenue. The anvil and bellows of the forge survive in The Fox public house.

The 1930s view of The Fox public house shows a very different appearance both at ground floor level and at the top of the gable.

The horse chestnut tree has given way to more car parking and Crowley's Croydon Ales have long since disappeared in favour of the products of Messrs Bass Charrington.

Both views look eastwards along Stites Hill Road on Coulsdon Common with the left-hand turning in the modern view being Homefield Road, close to Taunton Manor School.

The older photograph dates about 1912 and shows the Coulsdon windmill which was demolished in 1924.

COULSDON ROAD
OLD COULSDON
28
WALK
ST

This pair of photographs shows the development of garden trees and hedges in the Coulsdon Road over a period of more than fifty years.

Taken at the junction of Stoneyfield Road, the modern view is unusual in showing a traffic-free scene. The nearest drive-way belongs to number 41 Coulsdon Road.

Coulsdon Court is shown here as it appeared in 1908 and 1989. The Victorian mansion was built in 1850 and survived the threat of demolition a few years ago.

The refurbishment has incorporated the name of Byron from the family who had been the lords of the manor of Coulsdon for many years.

Marlpit Farm stands in splendid isolation in the early photograph which was taken in about 1912.

Marlpit Lane was widened in the late 1920s and the Farm survives as number 22. Note the house in Downs Road in the earlier view and Cane Hill Hospital may also be seen on the skyline.

A group of Edwardian schoolboys posing for a photographer in about 1905 contrasts sharply with the view of the modern Marlpit Lane over eighty years later. In the early years of this century, Marlpit Lane was a deeply rutted cart track with steep grassy banks leading to Bradmore Green, the village school and St. John's Parish Church.

Downs Road, which was originally Fanfare Road, is shown in the above photograph as it appeared in about 1910.

The modern view shows the access road to Farthing Downs and the houses visible are numbers 14-18 Downs Road.

Farthing Downs, Coulsdon.

The 1920s view of Farthing Downs is looking north-westwards and the development of Smitham Downs may be seen on the right.

In the modern photograph the camera is pointing towards Old Coulsdon and Purley High School for Girls can be seen on the skyline. The fencing behind the finger-post protects one of five saplings planted to restore the total to seven as shown in Thomas Bainbridge's map of 1783.

The northern slopes of Farthing Downs are shown here with the early view dating from about 1910.

The houses shown are numbers 34-40 Downs Road. There was considerable opposition to the metalling of the road across the downs in post-war years.

The imposing front entrance to Cane Hill Hospital is shown here with its ivy covering in about 1920 and in its modern, sanitised form. Note the handsome gas lamp in the earlier photograph.

Front Entrance — CANE HILL Asylum.

The Hospital was built in 1883 but is currently being phased out. Despite some recent planning applications for residential development, its future is still uncertain.

Coulsdon Station

Coulsdon South Station, Brighton Road, in 1904. Opened in 1889 by the South Eastern Railway Company to serve Cane Hill and Smitham Bottom from the main line, it was briefly given the misnomer Coulsdon East in 1923 when the Southern Railway was formed.

In 1989, Coulsdon South awaits an influx of commuters as plans for housing at Cane Hill are debated at a public enquiry.

Coulsdon from Stoats Nest Station.

L.B. &
STOAT
STAT

The Brighton Road has an entirely different appearance in the early view which dates from about 1905.

The road to the right led to Stoats Nest Station (later Coulsdon North) and there has been a small garden centre on this corner for some years. Note the neat hedge which has given way to the Coulsdon Library and a parade of shops.

Coulsdon Post Office is shown above as it appeared in 1910 when it was owned by Mr Carey. It had been extended from Claremont which was built in 1906.

Today, the little shop survives as a florist's in the Brighton Road opposite the Library. The building on the left of the modern view is the Comrades Club.

BRIGHTON ROAD, THE "OLD MAN'S CORNER", COULSDON.

61287.

Lion Green Road is shown here at its junction with Brighton Road. The early view dates from about 1925 when the nearest building to the camera was still Coppard's Temperance Hotel where cyclists could enjoy a drink under the shady tree.

The building has long since been used by an optician but the alterations shown in the modern photograph suggest that a different type of retail outlet is planned.

28

Chipstead Valley Road is pictured here looking towards Chipstead Valley School (hidden behind the tall tree on the left) at the junction with Gidd Hill.

The earlier view was taken in about 1929. A builder's hut can be seen at the centre of the photograph.

Sherwood Road in 1931 with a view of the railway which transformed the downland to the commuter dormitory we know today.

![Chipstead Valley Road](Chipstead valley Road. 2)

This view of Chipstead Valley Road opposite the primary school by How Lane was taken in 1922.

The railway bridge has carried trains on the Tattenham Corner line between Smitham and Chipstead Stations since its opening in 1897.

Chipstead Valley Road at Lion Green Road and Woodcote Grove Road in 1907 with Smitham School (Infants' Department) on the left.

This has become a busy junction, particularly since the opening of the M25, with traffic bound for Sutton leaving the Brighton Road at Lion Green.

Mrs Trish's corner shop which sold groceries, wines and spirits has for many years been used by an undertaker.

Coulsdon, Chipstead Road.

Chipstead (Valley) Road in 1906, with a more residential flavour than in 1989.

On the left, the flint-faced building, opened in 1893 as the Smitham Bottom Infants' School, is subject to preservation bids as a community facility. Rebuilding plans for the school off Portnalls Road, are in hand.

The earlier view of the Red Lion with its distinctive mansard roof dates from the 1920s. The building was replaced in 1927 and further re-built following bomb damage sustained in the last war.

Regular bus services started from here in 1914 but it is many years since The Red Lion was last used as a terminus.

Brighton Road, Coulsdon.

This view of Brighton Road, looking north from outside the Red Lion in 1911 shows a marked contrast to the traffic congested scene of 1989.

The horse chestnut tree in the early view was sadly cut down when the public conveniences were con-structed.

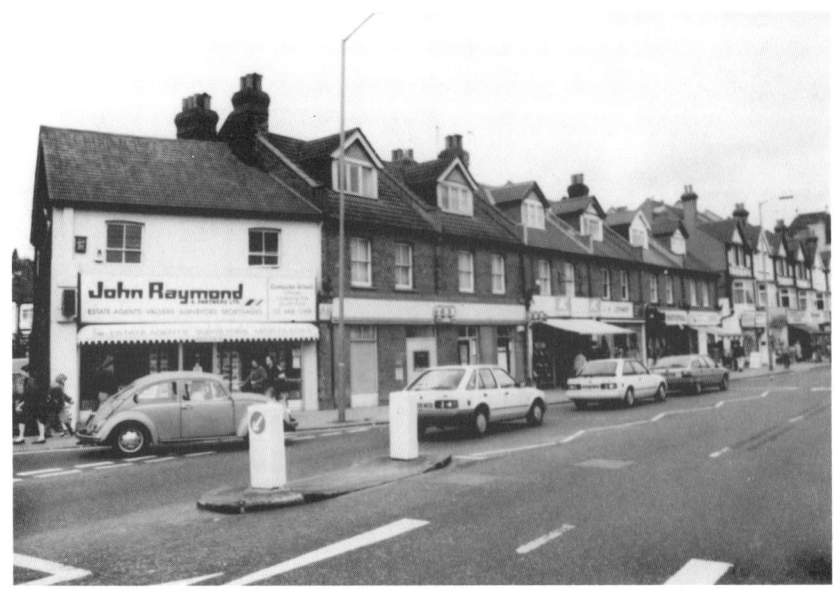

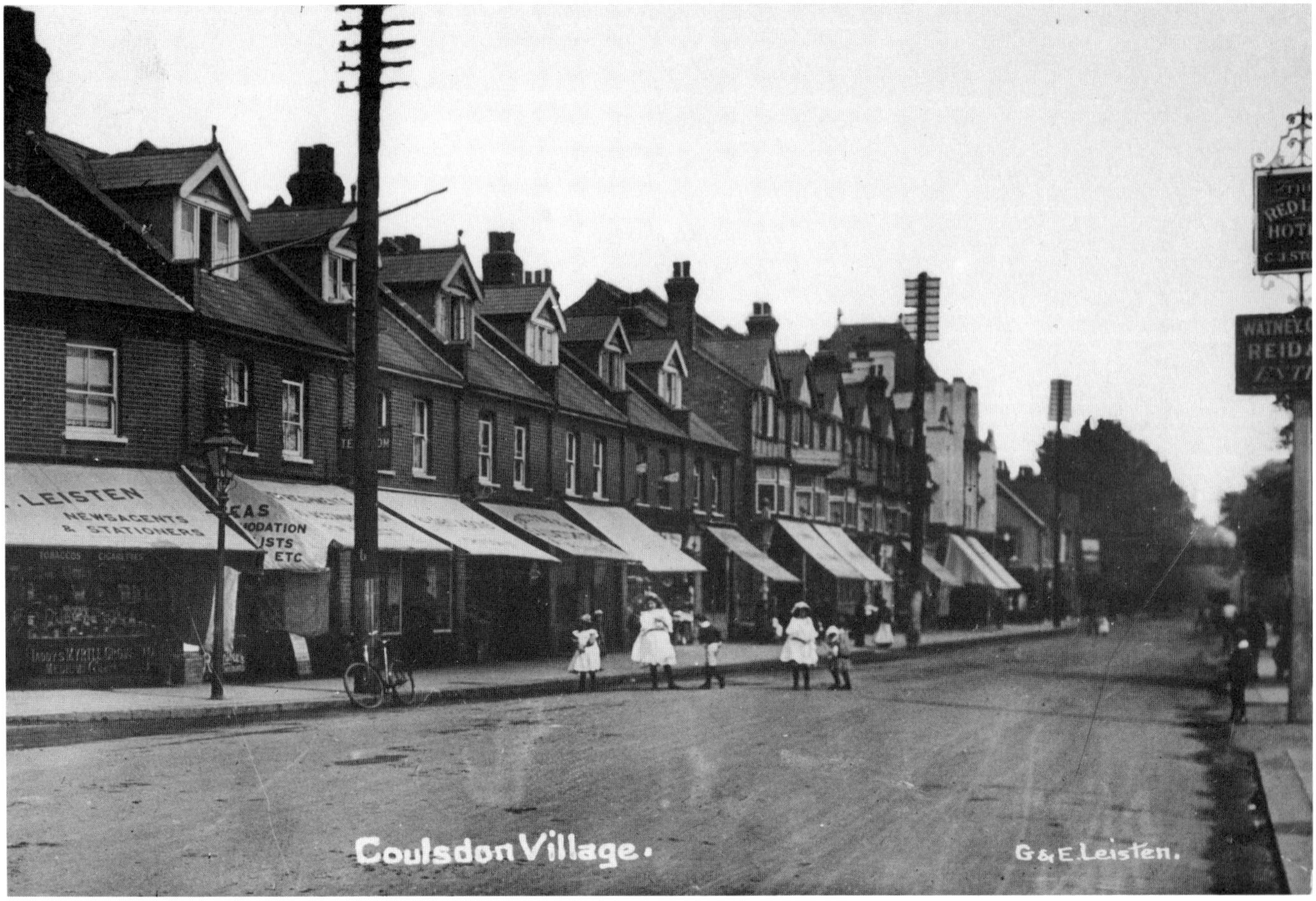
LEISTEN
NEWSAGENTS
& STATIONERS
Coulsdon Village.
G & E. Leisten.

The upper storeys of the shops in Brighton Road have changed very little since the early photograph was taken in about 1912.

John Raymond

The shop fronts though, have undergone several alterations and the road markings reflect the heavy volume of traffic at this junction with Chipstead Valley Road. The building in the distance is the modern Waitrose Supermarket, which replaced that of the Express Dairy.

Malcolm Road looking south-west in 1914.

In the modern view (near Waitrose Supermarket) the building on the left was used as a cinema for Smitham Bottom, where silent films were shown in instalments accompanied by violin or piano.

ST. ANDREW'S CHURCH, COULSDON.

61289.

St Andrew's Church is shown here at the junction of Woodcote Grove Road and Woodmansterne Road.

The early view was taken in about 1925 when the Church was still unfinished and it remained so until 1964 when it was completed - just in time for its golden jubilee. Before moving to this site, the Church had started its existence on the Brighton Road where the Comrades Club is now situated.

Woodcote Grove Road is shown here looking north at its junction with Woodmansterne Road and to the right, The Avenue.

The heavy traffic which now uses the road is a far cry from the gentle horse-drawn vehicles shown in the early view of about 1914. Note the uneven surface of the early roads and the small number of trees in the gardens.

Smitham Downs Road (which is now Purley) is shown looking south-east in about 1912 and in early 1989.

The bare downland in the distance has gradually been developed throughout the present century and, nearer to the camera, a fine display of trees and hedges has appeared although a few casualties from the great storm of October 1987 are evident.

Brighton Road, Coulsdon, looking north in 1937.

In 1989 there is a plan to build a roundabout for the proposed Coulsdon Bypass beyond the railway bridge. If this is done, Coulsdon may once more become tolerable for shoppers.

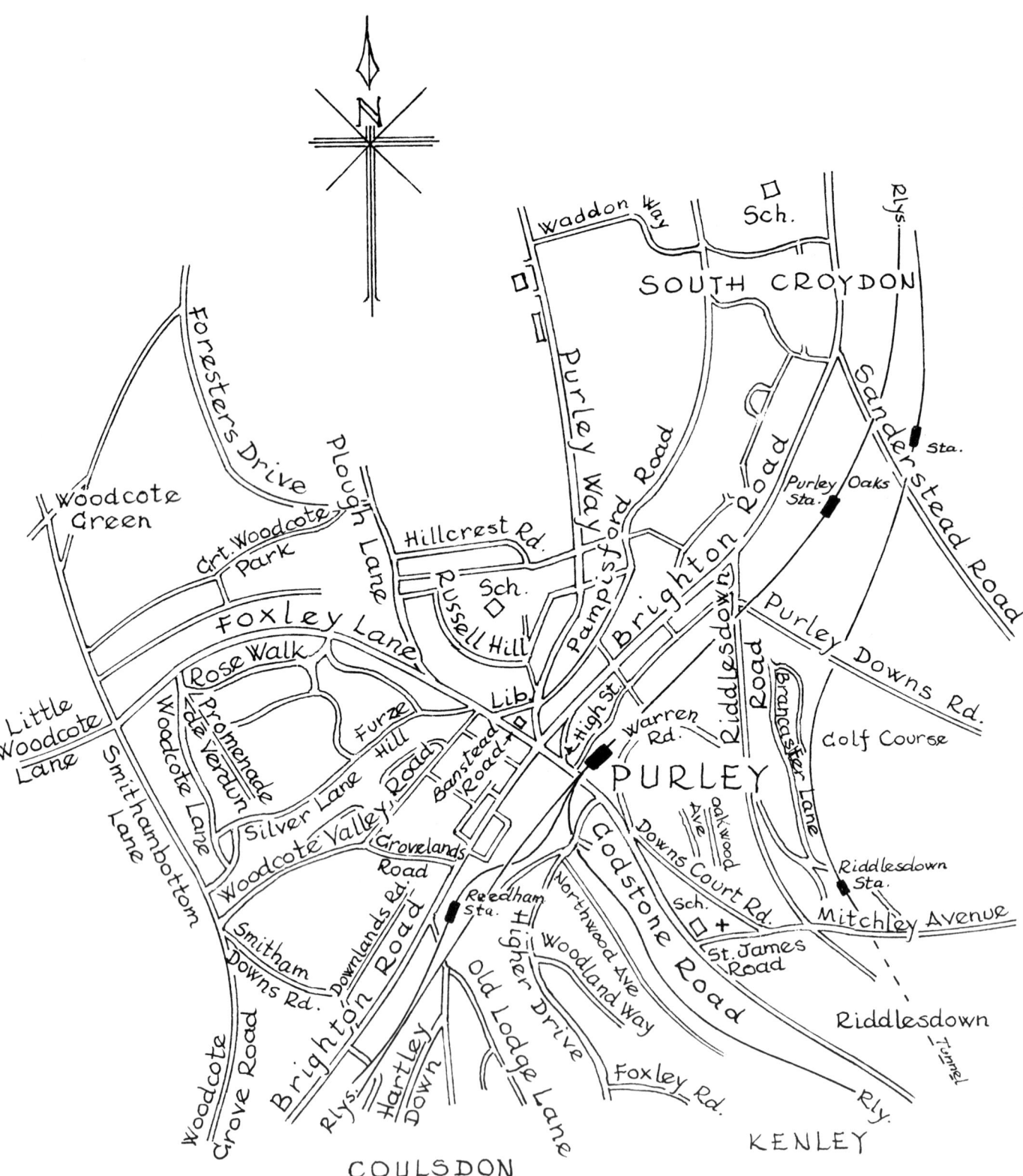

N

Woodcote Green

Foresters Drive

Plough Lane

Grt. Woodcote Park

Hillcrest Rd.

Waddon Way

Sch.

SOUTH CROYDON

Rlys.

Sta.

Sanderstead Road

Purley Way

Pampisford Road

Brighton Road

Purley Oaks Sta.

Foxley Lane

Rose Walk

Little Woodcote Lane

Promenade de Verdun

Woodcote Lane

Sch.

Russell Hill

Furze Hill

Lib.

High St.

Warren Rd.

PURLEY

Riddlesdown Road

Purley Downs Rd.

Brancaster Lane

Golf Course

Smithambottom Lane

Silver Lane

Banstead Road

Woodcote Valley Road

Grovelands Road

Godstone Road

Oakwood Ave

Downs Court Rd.

Riddlesdown Sta.

Mitchley Avenue

Smitham Downs Rd.

Downlands Rd.

Brighton Road

Reedham Sta.

Northwood Ave

Woodland Way

Sch.

St. James Road

Woodcote Grove Road

Rlys.

Hartley Down

Old Lodge Lane

Higher Drive

Foxley Rd.

Riddlesdown Tunnel

Rly.

KENLEY

COULSDON

42

Purley

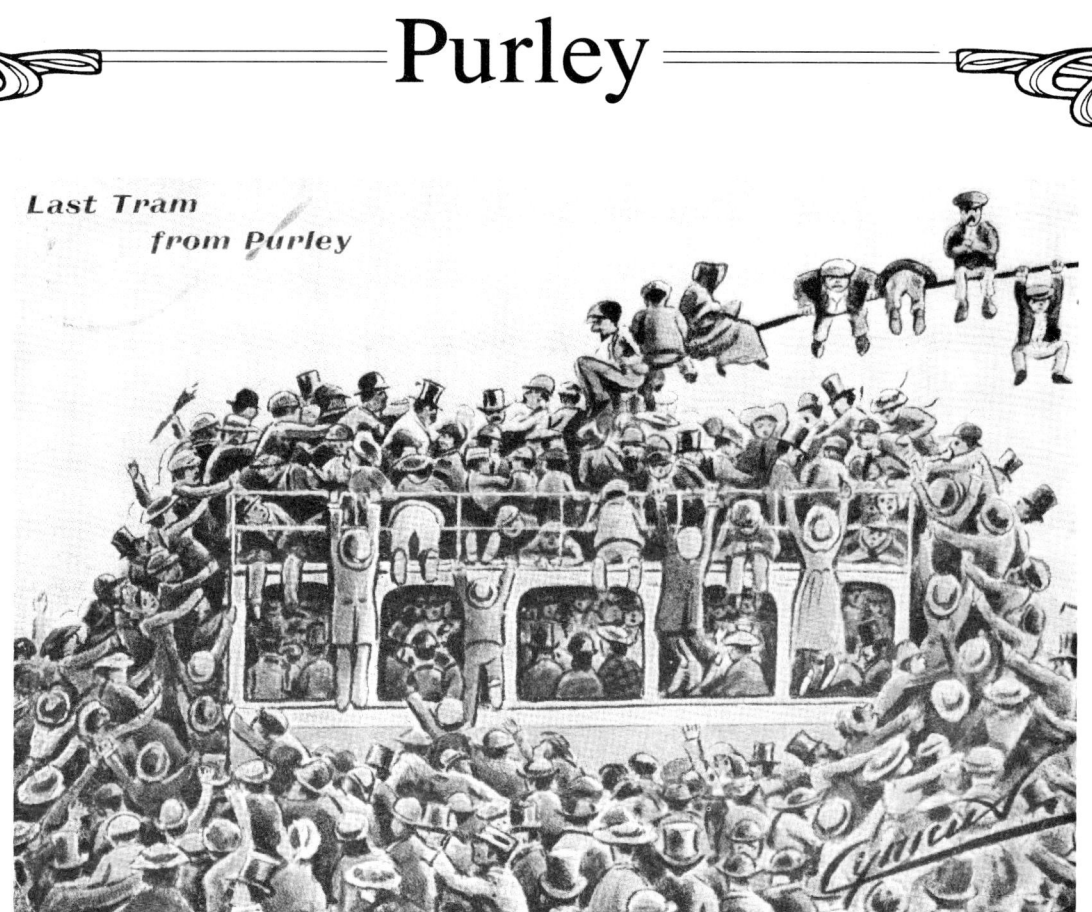

Last Tram from Purley

Purley was the end of the line for trams from central London and during Edwardian times they were very popular, bringing visitors to Riddlesdown and the delights of Gardners in Godstone Road. The last tram to Purley, returning to Thornton Heath, ran on April 7th. 1951.

PURLEY TRAM TERMINUS.

Brighton Road c.1904. From about 1880 a number of pleasant villas lined one side of the Brighton Road. On the corner of Russell Hill Road was Foxley Cottage, recalling the Foxley Hatch tollgate that stood nearby.

With the introduction of electric trams in 1901 the route was extended southwards from the Red Deer; the villas were demolished, and replaced by a bank and shops. This was the work of the local developer J.P. Oldaker, who also built Kimberley Terrace and Pretoria Terrace (1903) across the road. Today's scene lacks the tranquility of former days!

The Fountain, Purley.

The Fountain, Brighton Road c.1912. The triangle of land created by the road pattern was given by Vernon J. Watney for use as the site of the Queen Victoria Memorial Fountain, which was inaugurated by the Duchess of Albany on June 11th. 1904.

There is still a small triangle of grass where the fountain stood, on which are silver birch trees and a clock.

Queen Victoria Memorial Fountain, Purley

In 1904 the left side of the block which included one of Sainsbury's earliest shops was not yet completed.

In the Spring of 1989 a short stretch of the Brighton Road to the left of this view was widened, creating an extra traffic lane.

Purley — near Croydon

The fountain was enclosed by five foot high spiked railings. Water, supplied by Croydon Corporation, also fed a public drinking fountain and a horse trough.

In March 1935, with the installation of traffic lights, the fountain was moved a few yards southwards nearer to Purley waterworks to which it was then connected. A low brick surround and seats on which to rest and watch the passing traffic completed the new landscaping.

In the 1950s the fountain was again threatened by traffic and came near to being scrapped. However, the East Surrey Water Company came to the rescue and placed it in the grounds of their Purley waterworks. In 1983, as part of their Diamond Jubilee celebrations, the Purley Rotary Club instigated the fountain's third move, this time into the grounds of Purley Library, where it is hoped it has found a permanent site.

Purley Road c.1905.

Purley Road, bounded on the left from 1901 by the grounds of the waterworks, has since become a vital link road in the modern system.

In the early 1930s the fountain was still on its original site and traffic passed in both directions on all sides. The houses built on Russell Hill Road lasted rather longer than those on the nearby Brighton Road as redevelopment did not take place until 1936.

When the corner of Purley Road with Brighton Road was redeveloped, a house was demolished. The other half of that semi-detached pair remains beside the Jolly Farmers but is not immediately recognisable as having once been an ordinary house. Sainsbury's shop moved to modern premises in the High Street in 1981.

Purley Road c.1904. The Jolly Farmers, established originally in a very rural setting, had a weatherboarded main block until it was rebuilt in about 1907. The noise from the smithy which used to be at the rear gave rise to its nickname of the 'Hammer and clink'!

Today a constant stream of traffic passes the door with huge lorries replacing the horse-drawn wagons of the more leisurely years.

The Exchange, Purley.

The Exchange, Purley Road c.1909. The Exchange, a block of shops with accommodation above, was built in 1908. The Council had been looking for a site for public conveniences, and these were erected at the rear of this block, with an access pathway on either side.

These were closed several years ago, having no doubt become costly to maintain, and the site has been redeveloped. The Exchange has changed very little.

PURLEY FROM THE STATION.

Purley Road and the High Street, looking north-west c.1906. The bare hillside has long been built over and the fronts of houses on the road by the bridge converted to shops.

Following the transfer to Kenley, the waterworks site, which opened in 1903, is now largely deserted, as is the corner site, occupied by the Railway Hotel. It closed in 1984, and was demolished in 1987.

Railway Hotel c.1905. Hotels were built at both ends of the branch railway line along the Caterham Valley when it opened in 1856, and both have been demolished. This one, originally called Caterham Junction, after the railway station, had a large triangular shaped frontage but this was built over about 1905 obscuring the lower part of the façade.

At some future date shall we find an office block on this prime site, or will it be another hotel?

54

Two further views of the Railway Hotel taken shortly before it was demolished in 1987.

A photograph taken in 1979 records that the flat roof behind the dome was a useful place to dry the washing!

High Street c.1903. These buildings at the end of the High Street opposite the Railway Hotel were built about 1870. Mafeking Terrace, built by J.P. Oldaker, still stands on the left of the High Street but the Public Elementary School (1889) has gone.

The redevelopment of the corner site was carried out about 1930, around the same time as the block containing the cinema (orginally the 'Astoria') was built.

High Street c.1905. This old High Street building still stands after nearly 120 years! The name Morgan can be seen on the sunblind, and this family business was here from 1896 to 1979.

'Cards' now have Morgan's premises, and an estate agent has taken Parker's shop. An old right of way passes between this block and the next, giving access to Whytecliffe Road and the station.

Purley Station c.1908. The railway station, called Godstone Road, opened in 1841 but was closed due to lack of custom.

It reopened in 1856 as Caterham Junction and in 1888 it became Purley.

Purley Station in about 1910 shows a Wainwright 'D' class, 4-4-0 steam engine No. 92 on platform 6. It was built in 1903 and withdrawn in 1951. A similar class engine may be seen at the railway museum at York. The other engine is serving either the Caterham or Tadworth branch line and is a Stirling class Q, 0-4-4T built between 1881 and 1897.

This recent view of Purley station from platforms 4 & 5 shows several changes including the modern lighting and signalling equipment and the modernised canopies. Platform 5 has been re-aligned to lessen the curve and the wooden platform boards have been replaced. The train waiting at platform 3 is a modern 2 × 4 CIG stock.

A plaque, presented by the Bourne Society, commemorates the re-naming of the station in 1888. The date 1899, when the station was rebuilt appears on the main façade.

The station master's house at Purley, was built soon after the station was opened in 1899. The house, pictured here in 1983, was pulled down to make way for a modern office block, which was completed in 1984. The building now houses the main local office of the Department of Employment.

On the south side of Whytecliffe road between numbers 16 & 18 is this small pathway which backs on to platform 1 of Purley station. In 1920 when this photograph was taken, the staff posing in the doorways were employed by the building firm of W. Saker.

A recent view shows several changes! The building on the right is now a showroom for a pine furnishing company. At number 16a a plaque on the wall states 'Formerly The Old Rulemakers Workshop'.

In 1983 the High Street housed the telephone exchange which was demolished later that year to make way for the shopping and office complex named Venture House.

Boots the Chemist moved here from Russell Hill in 1985.

This view of the High Street was taken in 1981. The Purley 'Uplands' telephone exchange seen on the right of the photograph was built in 1914.

The Venture House office and shopping complex was completed in 1985. The clock tower was originally part of the old public elementary school opened in 1889 and the developers rebuilt the tower on the original site. A plaque on the new end wall states 'This room was erected by special subscriptions in memory of John Henry Smith of Purleybury as a Church Room for Christ Church Purley 1889'.

The Congregational Church in the Brighton Road was built in 1902.

The church was renamed Purley United Reformed in 1972 and apart from minor alterations to the building, has changed little in the last eighty years.

Opening Ceremony, Purley Cottage Hospital, by Princess Christian, March 31st 1909.   copyright. W. Burdekin

Purley Cottage Hospital in Brighton Road was opened by Princess Christian on the 31st March 1909.

The hospital, which has served the district well for eighty years, closed its casualty department in March 1989. The out-patients department in the new wing on the right of the photograph was opened in 1940.

The tram terminus in Brighton Road c.1928. On the right hand side of the picture is the showroom of the Croydon Gas Company which opened its premises here in the early 1920s.

Despite rumours of closure over the last few years British Gas still occupies this site. Tram lines have long since been removed from the Brighton Road where motor traffic queues to get through Purley crossroads.

Brighton Road c.1932. The building on the left was built in 1928.

This modern view with minimum traffic shows little change apart from the growth of trees. New style Telecom phone booths have been installed outside the travel agents' premises which were for many years a ladies outfitters known as Gilwins.

Brighton Road, Purley.

Croydon Corporation Tram No. 46 is shown as it approaches the terminus in about 1912. It was built in 1902 by G.F. Milnes & Co for a cost of £825 and had 69 seats which remained uncovered upstairs until the late 1920s. Subsequently re-numbered 365, it was withdrawn in 1936.

The buildings on the left-hand side of the modern photograph were completed in 1928.

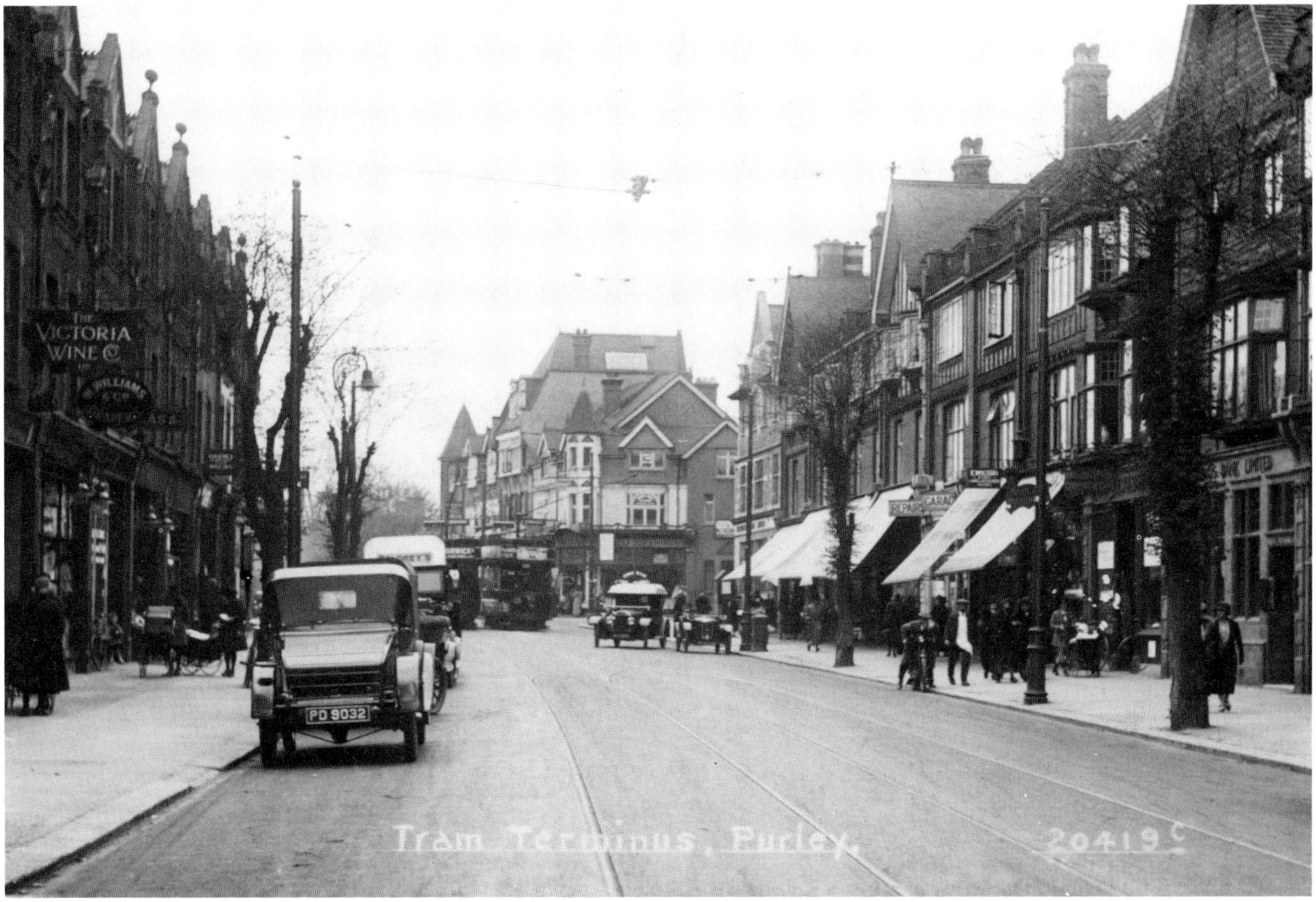

Brighton Road c.1923 when there were no yellow lines to deter passing motorists! On the right hand side at no. 954 the sunblind shielded the window display of Swattons, later Grants, who closed their Purley shop in 1986.

Apart from the increase in traffic and closure of many of the original shops, the outline of this part of Purley remains unchanged.

Brighton Road c.1923 was then pleasant for shoppers and the few passing motorists.

Kimberley Terrace on the left of the picture was built in 1903. The name commemorates the Boer war. Its roof tops remain virtually unchanged but many premises have changed hands.

The tram terminus c.1910. On the right of the picture stands Kimberley Terrace with the original premises of the Croydon Gas Company, now occupied by the ladies dress shop, Holder Bros.

On the left of this picture is the old Sainsbury's premises, from which they moved to the High Street in 1981. The premises remain unoccupied in 1989!

In the 1930s there were shops only on the south side of Russell Hill. Private houses still occupied the north side. The picture shows the Post Office as it was. The premises now belong to an Insurance Agent.

The road carried two-way traffic, to and from Purley Way, which was opened in 1924 as a bypass for Croydon and to service Croydon Airport.

In 1989, a one-way Russell Hill Road, now with business premises on both sides of the road, carries heavy traffic towards the M23 and M25. Woolworths closed in 1985 and Boots has moved to the new High Street development.

The South side of Russell Hill Road c.1930.

The houses were demolished in 1936-7, and the present shopping premises were built in 1937-8.

Russell Hill School, orginally the Warehousemen and Clerks School was opened by the Prince of Wales on June 18th. 1866. Its purpose was to provide education and board for orphans and for needy children of Warehousemen and Clerks. In 1885 the children of Drapers' were also included.

Early in the 1960s it ran into financial difficulties and the school moved to the Ballards Farm site where the Royal Russell School is today.

PURLEY, RUSSELL HILL SCHOOL, FROM SOUTH EAST

The Russell Hill site and buildings were eventually sold for £125,000 to the Roman Catholic Schools Commission under whose aegis it has since operated. There are now two schools here, the Thomas More School and the Margaret Roper Primary School. Both are classed as Voluntary Aided Schools.

Warehousemen Clerks and Drapers' Schools, Purley.
The Domestic Science Room.

The Domestic Science Room of the old Warehousemen, Clerks and Drapers' School built in the 1890s has been replaced by a Home Economics Room for the Thomas More High School. Note the use of the computer in the modern picture.

The Dining Hall of the Russell Hill School built over a century ago is little changed in structure, but is now the Main Hall of the Thomas More High School.

It has here been set up as an examination room.

These contrasting views of Foxley Lane show the junction with Woodcote Valley Road and Furze Lane to the right. The top photograph was taken in about 1905 and on the left-hand side can be seen the house 'Browside', now an old peoples' home.

The pleasing development of a variety of trees helps to compensate for the unforeseen increase in the local traffic.

Junction of Foxley Lane and Plough Lane c.1910.

Although this modern view shows very little traffic, it is normally a busy junction.

The Rose Walk & Promenade de Verdun, Purley.

Junction of Rose Walk and Promenade de Verdun c.1950.

This is part of the Webb estate, designed by William Webb in 1907.

The Lombardy Poplars along this grass walk were planted in Reverent Memory of those Brave Soldiers of France who fell in the Great War. The Ministry of the Interior has given earth from a sacred spot in the neighbourhood of Armentieres, so that each tree may grow in a combination of French and British soil.

The Public are asked to assist in protecting this arboricultural tribute.

Promenade de Verdun was laid out after the 1914-18 War, as described on the plaque.

The trees suffered in the hurricane of October 1987 and the promenade was completely replanted early in 1989.

"The Lord Roberts" Model Village, Upper Woodcote 21/9/06

The 'Lord Roberts' Temperance Inn at Upper Woodcote Village Green in 1906, showing Mr. Charles Wakeling's ducks by the Model Village pond.

Mr Wakeling's forge was nearby, in which much of the ironwork for Upper Woodcote Estate was made between 1904 and 1914.

Interior view of Lord Roberts Temperance Inn, Woodcote Green in 1910, contrasting with the General Stores and Sub-Post Office of today.

The shop is now owned by Mr. Ron Mathews.

Purley Knoll looking towards the Brighton Road c.1908. The water-works site is in the centre of the picture with Downs Court Road and Riddlesdown in the distance.

Today's view shows little change except for the matured trees, and the road has an 'open plan' appearance.

Brighton Road c.1912, looking towards the Purley crossroads with Purley Knoll on the left.

The Brighton Road has at this point, lost many of its trees. A new traffic lane has been added on the right hand side and was completed in March 1989, although the photograph was taken before work had started.

BRIGHTON ROAD, PURLEY,
SHOWING COUNCIL OFFICES, AMBULANCE STATION, SKATING RINK, SITE FOR CINEMA - OLD LODGE LANE.

Brighton Road c.1935, with the Council Offices on the left of the picture. They were built in 1930 for what was then the Coulsdon and Purley Urban District Council.

The Skating Rink and Cinema are now a Dance Hall and Bingo Hall. The junction with Old Lodge Lane is at the traffic lights, in the middle of the picture.

REEDHAM LANE, PURLEY. (3061)

Looking along what is now known as Old Lodge Lane, from the Brighton Road towards Reedham Halt. c.1912.

The most obvious changes are the road widening and the modern street furniture.

The Reedham Orphanage, Purley

Reedham Orphanage in 1908, was established in Purley by Andrew Reed in 1858 as the Asylum for Fatherless Children and was known as Reedham School from 1950 until its closure in 1979.

It has been replaced by a modern housing development of the type which is changing the character of the district.

THE REEDHAM ORPHANAGE, PURLEY, SURREY.

A view of Old Lodge Lane in 1908, showing the farmland setting of Reedham's 'six acre field'.

Reedham Orphanage and School has given way to the Reedham Trust.

This charity still helps children in need and the trust operates from the lodge at the corner of Reedham Drive and Old Lodge Lane.

This interesting view of Old Lodge Lane in about 1912 shows the partially developed hills of west Purley and Smitham Downs.

The houses, which are now numbers 57-67 enjoy an unimpeded view towards Hartley Down. Beyond the furthest house is the right-hand turn into Burcott Road.

GODSTONE ROAD.

Godstone Road c.1908 looking south, with Dale Road on the right and Downs Court Road in the distance.

The three pairs of houses in the photograph were demolished in the early 1960s to make way for the Downs Court Road roundabout, which has never been built. The space has become a car park. Dr. Lindsay's house was in the garden on the right. The Lister Court Flats were built here in 1963.

Godstone Road c.1912 at the junction of Downs Court Road and Warren Road.

This modern view is deceptively quiet for what is a very busy junction.

The houses on the right of the old view have long since been demolished and the Dale Road car park has taken their place.

Foxley Hill from the Cliffe c.1912, with Foxley Hall in the background.

Today, due to the growth of trees, the same view is almost impossible so our photograph was taken from Warren Road. The Dale Road car park has replaced the Edwardian houses in the old photograph.

Godstone Road c.1910 with Purley railway bridge in the distance.

The shops in the Foxley Parade have undergone many changes over nearly eighty years and the railway bridge in the distance was rebuilt in 1983.

Purley fountain c.1907
The lady with the pram would find it very difficult to cross Purley Road today!

The traffic roars past the old site of Purley fountain with hardly time to notice the clock donated by the Rotary Club.

The fountain in Purley c.1911

The fountain and its adjacent horse trough must have been a welcome sight for the drivers of the horses and carts that passed through this junction. Some of the drivers no doubt called at the Jolly Farmers!

In 1988 Croydon Council proposed a major flyover at this crossroads to divert the A23 trunk road traffic away from the centre of Purley. The plan was not approved and we await future proposals to save the centre of the town from traffic strangulation!

Brighton Road c.1910

Looking towards Coulsdon, the waterworks site on the left awaits redevelopment. The road widening on the left hand side was completed early in 1989.

Russell Hill, Purley.

Our final view of Purley was taken in the vicinity of Coldharbour Lane c.1907.
The Edwardian gentleman could have had no idea how the town would change over the following eighty years and perhaps we should now contemplate what changes may take place before the end of this century!

INDEX

This provides an index to the main streets, buildings etc. in Coulsdon and Purley but does not include every establishment due to lack of space.

COULSDON

Bradmore Green	10, 20
Brighton Road	7, 26, 27, 28, 32, 35, 36, 38, 41
Cane Hill	7, 19, 24, 25
Chipstead Station	31
Chipstead Valley Rd	29, 31, 32, 33, 36
Coulsdon Common	14, 16
Coulsdon Court	18
Coulsdon Road	8, 13, 14, 17
Dormer Lodge	11
Downs Road	19, 21, 23
Fanfare Road	21
Farthing Downs	19, 21, 22, 23
Fox	14, 15
Gidd Hill	29
Grange Park	11
Homefield Road	16
How Lane	14
Lacey Green	14
Lion Green Road	28, 32
Malcolm Road	37
Marlpit Lane	19, 20
Old Coulsdon	7
Placehouse Lane	13
Portnalls Road	33
Post Office	8, 9, 10, 27
Red Lion	34, 35
St. Andrew's Church	38
St. John's Church	7, 11, 12, 20
Sherwood Road	30
Smitham Bottom	25, 37
Smitham Downs Road	40
Smitham School	32
Station	25, 26
Stites Hill Road	16
Stoneyfield Road	17
Taunton Manor School	16
Tudor Estate	13
Tudor Rose	13
Waddington Avenue	13
Waitrose	36, 37
Woodcote Grove Road	32, 38, 39
Woodmansterne Road	38, 39

PURLEY

Astoria Cinema	56
Boots	62, 72
Brighton Road	44, 45, 46, 48, 50
	64, 65, 66, 67, 68
	69, 70, 71, 82, 83
	84, 94
Browside	76
Burcott Road	87
Cliff End	90
Coldharbour Lane	95
Congregational Church	64
Cottage Hospital	65
Council Offices	83
Dale Road	88, 89, 90
Downs Court Road	81, 89
Exchange	52
Fountain	45, 46, 47, 48, 50, 92, 93
Foxley Hill	90
Foxley Lane	76, 77
Foxley Parade	91
Furze Lane	76
Godstone Road	43, 55, 58, 89, 91
Hospital	65
Jolly Farmers	50, 51, 93
Kimberley Terrace	44, 70, 71
Library	48
Lord Roberts	79, 80
Mafeking Terrace	56
Margaret Roper School	74
Morgan's	57
Old Lodge Lane	83, 84, 86, 87
Parkers	57
Plough Lane	77
Pretoria Terrace	44
Promenade de Verdun	78
Purley Knoll	81, 82
Purley Road	49, 50, 51, 52, 53
Railway Hotel	53, 54, 55, 56
Reedham Lane	84
Reedham Orphanage	85, 86
Reedham School	85, 86
Reedham Station	84, 86
Rose Walk	78
Russell Hill Road	44, 50, 72, 73, 74, 95
Sainsbury's	46, 50, 71
Station	58, 59, 60, 61
Thomas More School	74, 75
United Reformed Church	64
Upper Woodcote Village Green	79, 80
Venture House	62, 63
Warehousemens School	74
Warren Road	89, 90
Waterworks	47, 48, 49, 53, 81, 94
Webb Estate	78
Whytecliffe Road	57, 61
Woodcote Valley Road	76
Woolworths	72